UNDERSTORY

poems by **Paulann Petersen**

UNDERSTORY

LOST HORSE PRESS
Sandpoint, Idaho

Cover Art: Barbara Mason
    Solar Plate Intaglios by print maker Barbara Mason may be viewed on line at
    www.barbara-mason.com.

Author Photo: Sabina Samiee
    Photographs by Sabina Samiee may be viewed online at www.sabinasamiee.com.

Cover & Book Design: Christine Holbert

This and other fine LOST HORSE PRESS titles may be viewed online at www.losthorsepress.org.

FIRST EDITION

Library of Congress Cataloging-in-Publication Data

Petersen, Paulann.
  Understory : poems / by Paulann Petersen.—First edition.
     p: cm
  ISBN 978-0-9883166-2-1 (alk. paper)
  I. Title.
  PS3566.E7636U55 2013
  811'.54—dc23
                        2012051476

TABLE OF CONTENTS

I An Underworld's Dust

1 Daily Cosmology

2 Bequeathed

3 What Little I Know of Grief's Emblem

4 Idol

5 Architecture

6 Synesthesia

7 Living in Pain

8 Ascent

9 In Good Time

10 Shape-Shifter

12 Drowse

II The Sound of Another Heart

15 My Father's Voice

16 What Memory Is

17 Perspective

18 Remedy

20 Of the Light That Would Change My Life

21 Coming Around

22 Along Seven Mile Creek

23 Threshold

25 39 Being the Average Age of Enlightenment, or So I'm Told

26 Estrangement

28 For My Portrait Painter, a Request to Consider
   What Van Gogh Did for Eugene Bloch

29 On the Side of My House Painted Blue

30 Solder

32 In the World Lying Worlds Below

33 From the Very Start

34 A Place at Her Table

36 In Motion

37 Night Storm

III Flash of Pollen

41 A Prothalamion

42 Plate Set before Us

43 And Justly So

44 Letters Toward the End

45 It Just So Happens Today I'm Tired of

46 Sympathy for a Friend Not Entirely Bereaved

47 Last Tongue

48 Widows

49 One Work of This Earth

50 An Atlas of Taste

51 Paying Attention

53 Early in the Ocean's Present Life, You Appear

54 Capital

55 Remembering My Copy of *A Glass Face in the Rain* Was Long Ago Borrowed and Never Returned

56 Why the Aging Poet Continues to Write

57 Airborne

IV Shimmer and Drone

61 Beginning with 'And'

62 The World Begins This Every Instant

63 Exhalation

64 White Noise, Yellow Dust

66 The Tabla Player

67 Vespers in Anhdra Pradesh

68 Worship Requires You to Jolt the God Awake

69 Raga

70 Of the Heat That Broods This World

71 As for the Appeal of a Certain Avatar's
    Sweet Androgynous Looks

72 Indian Miniatures

73 Evaporation

74 Transported

V

A Same Sky

77 Raiment

78 The Silence After

80 Where You Began Your Singing

83 The Village Dyer Makes Widow's Weeds

84 Aubade

85 Cyprus

86 From the Wholly Horizontal

87 Last Night, When She Seemed Asleep

88 At a Wishing Spring on a Turkish Mountainside
    Miles above the Black Sea

89 Why, of Renoir's Works, His Floral Bouquets Interest
    Me the Least

90 Set to Rise

91 As Noted in Museums of Note

93 How Frida Kahlo Speaks of Color

95 The Cave Painter's Manifesto

96 Out of Season

97 Playa Publico

98 A Colonial Translation

99 Elsewhere

100 Interment

101 So Spirit Will Live in Our Midst

VI *Half Heaven*

105 Legacy

106 The Moon in Her Phases

107 Straw into Gold

109 The Moon Reveals How Certain Coats Get Their Gleam

110 Notions

111 Four of the Stargazers

113 Guise

114 Rose White Tells Her Story

116 Alchemy

117 Lethe's Poppy

118 The Moon Recounts the Birth of the Sun

120 Death Mask

121 The Mother Who Became a Tree

122 Danae Recalls Her Undoing

123 Kin

VII *Telltale*

127 André Breton Shares His Muse

128 Integument

129 Calendars

130 His Translator Speaks to Pessoa

131 Blue Bee, Your Ancient Cult Convening

132 REM

133 Ode to My Magpie

134 Three Words Recollect Their Earlier Selves

135 Flux

136 Recluse

137 Before the Wake Can End

138 From the Fire at the House's Heart

139 While a Coneflower's Orange Florets Sharpen the Air

140 To the River Living a Few Blocks Away

141 In Beauty's Eye

142 As If Each Breath Were the Last

143 When Spirit Transforms the Body

VIII *Darkly Lit Blood*

147 For the Silence Among and Around Words

148 A Floor Plan

149 Morning

150 Insight

151 Font

152 Coda

153 Bedside Reading

154 How to Vanish into Today's Sky

155 Here to Wait Out the Dark

156 Imprint

157 Why the Astilbe's Color Fades

158 Interchangeable

159 Light Finds You

160 To the Milky Way

161 Balance

IX *The Furrier's Next of Kin*

165 Keep

166 Showroom

168 What the Shaman Knew, What My Grandfather the Furrier
     Wouldn't Have Known to Do with the Whole Otterskin
     Used as a Medicine Bag:

169 Trophy

170 A Recipe for Abstention

171 Mechanistics

173 Pastoral

174 Transaction

175 Conversion

176 Pawnee Star-Chart

177 Migratory

178 Direction

180 To Merely Look, to Pass on By

181 If Ever I Learn to Fly

182 And Where Does It Come from, This Animal Soul?

for Ken

I

An Underworld's Dust

A tree names itself *Creation*, and having done so,
reaches above, yet never breaks
the horizon's line. Its trunk
makes a vertical road, way for a voyage
of ascent. Its mouths—would I argue
a tree is lacking mouths? have I looked
so little, been that inattentive?—the mouths of the tree
bloom. Breath leaves those lips
as a fine, yellow dust. This is the truth
I *did* realize, all along. Each dawn,
a tree's pollen breathes
our world into being.

BEQUEATHED

Morning. This neighborhood,
unearthly still. The sun is dying—
gone to heaven, leaving its light.
Including us in its estate, the sun
wills us to rise and thrive.

Each day our star lights us
awake. Each night, its absence
serves as our reminder. In dark sky
we see the sun's countless kin,
the world—*our* world—
minus what keeps us alive.

WHAT LITTLE I KNOW OF GRIEF'S EMBLEM

Dark taper, you cast off
a sheen where every needle
chafes against light.

Tree of dim branches
never spreading out,
you grow higher than even
my dreams trying you on
for size.

Neighborhood ornamental,
you're named *Cypress*,
the one chosen to make
a long unbroken shade.

Reaching straight down,
your taproot would mirror
the length of your trunk
could I look inward
that far and see
you feeding on what lies
hidden below.

Wrought from deepness,
your shadow-green needles
stay powdered
with an underworld's dust.

No wind of this upper realm
will ever dislodge
that film from your limbs—
the pale ash
you steal from buried bone.

IDOL

A mirror could be made
perfectly round
to represent the Sun—
this time with a capital *S*
because it's divine.

Given a chance to reflect
a little light from the everyday
lowercase sun,
the mirror would then
accept prayers.
Huge jewel above an altar,
that mirror would shine.

How like its lesser,
half-sister. How like the moon.

The sun's the one who starts it—
this struggle some call a war
between himself and the moon.
Suddenly he's busy strong-arming
a stretch of mud until it glazes over
like a silky quilt, crazing like
a checkerboard. His chosen site
a decided plane, he takes timbers,
glass and steel—those building blocks
wrought with his master builder's heat—
and contrives them into increment,
high and dry as the swept-out sky.
Stringer, baffle, joist and shim,
they all please him who banks on
altitude as investment, who rises
in the binding light of foreseeable
futures—this sun who's set
on outranking, outflanking the moon.

What can she do? Pale, desirous—
what else but pull, with a mere sliver
of her borrowed light, oceans of water
from here to there, then back again.
Stream, swamp and eddy sent to loosen
a builder's dreams, to cast his work
into settle and shift, to watery crumble.
She sighs, she dwindles, she holds
her breath. She grows and grows full—
swollen on slow dissolution.

SYNESTHESIA

Be a leaf, learn
to eat with your skin,
swallowing sun's rankness
wherever it strikes you.

Savor light, that mother
to every sweetness.
Become the bee's green sister,
the one who can taste
this world with her hands.

Money is useless here.
Whatever you pull from your pocket
is turned away. No door
exists to a place of welcome,
only windows through which you peer
into other lives.

A woman bends to the shape
of routine, the food she prepares
having so much smell
or so little smell, it consumes
all the air either way.

Sparrows perch in trees
with unfamiliar sharpness,
their markings too brown, too gray.
They sing in tongues.

You remember the grandfather,
tongue-tied at birth,
how a doctor cut the membrane
that held his speech.

Here, in this foreign place,
this country of the body
where everyone is native born,
you are the tongue-tied,
waiting for the knife
to free your voice.

ASCENT

A birch tree is bare
of its lower branches.
Seven oozing limb-stumps make
seven steps toward the sky,
the upper branches extending
above any roofline's peak.

Climbing, you discover
no top, no leafy crest
to cradle you as you sway.
Just ever and ever more ascent
pulling you upward until
you discover you're only bones,
a template of shape
for remaking yourself
after you climb back down—

your feet sticky with pitch, your hands
this terrible amber, gleaming.

Something with tree-big bones—
a thing with leaves,
a forest bulk
with acres of dark understory—
crowds in,
rides the air into me
as I inhale.

Its moss-crusted skeleton
stays inside me
when I breathe out.

A whiff of pathos
hovers around me,
stinging the cave of my throat.

What all
do I breathe for now?
Better breathe deep.

Something with bones
too clumsy—
so heavy it won't be moved
by prayer or practice
or twelve-step plodding—
moves in for good.

This heft foreseen
too long ago to ever
leave on its own accord.

SHAPE-SHIFTER

The mother of one of the marrying women
will turn out to be *her father,*
now a woman, who wears her long gray hair pulled away
from her bone-shadowed face
to hang in a fall down her spine.
Below a hint of breasts, the skirt of her dress
drapes off her belly-slope
to end, swaying, above her ankles.
She says to me, taking my hand, "Kate is my daughter,"
and I take her as saying "I'm Kate's mother."
Thinking *tall, so tall to be Kate's mother.*
Not thinking, but knowing
how old women and old men grow to look like both,
I see *dress, long hair, barrettes,*
old-woman-belly, I see Kate's
mother, an elder woman making her stiff-stepped way
across the living room after the wedding,
speaking to each guest.

A woman has married another woman
here, today. Hosanna!
Unthinkable in my life's early years—and I think
We people have finally learned
something. I will not learn until days from now
that the mother of one of the brides
is really her father
changed as a shaman might change
to be able to step near spirits
without frightening them away.
The day I learn, bees will be out, working blossoms.
A breeze, out moving leaves. On a day
blind-blue with the sun's shine,

a sparrow will clatter in a gutter, spooling
clutter to make a nest. Stunned,
I will *see*—for a moment—
how every shape in our green world
is indeed a father,
is a mother giving a child away,
giving away to *shimmer*,
away to endless *shift*.

DROWSE

Nowadays, the god has disappeared
into sleep, reaching out—
right now—to pull your eyelids down.
Your eyes blink—you're here,
not here. They're open, then not.
Weight drains awareness
away, gathers it into
the pool beneath.

This water is a darkness
where the dead cajole
and see through disguise
in one swift glance.
Taking you in, their eyes have
taken you in. There, deep—
among the living and dead
who are no longer
either/or, but both—
you're afloat in the god's
iris-pool.

II

The Sound of Another Heart

MY FATHER'S VOICE

Caught on tape, its dappled gleam
makes a brief but vivid swim
upstream through time—him, long dead,
telling me his story. Still a boy, he's in a line
of hired hands on horseback
strung across a Montana river.
Guiding their cow ponies against the flow,
they drag a net behind them
through snow-melt,
seining for fish.

They're men far from home, miles
from a rod, boat or the flat, deep water
fit for its launch. High-country horsemen
with a yen for trout sizzled crisp
by bacon grease bubbling
in a cast iron pan.
                    I'm still that girl
hungry for her father's talk—
him caught on a minute of shining
magnetic tape. On the wide-cast
net of longing.

WHAT MEMORY IS

Water, the glass to hold it,
lips, mouth, thirst,
the throat swallowing,
each cell bathed in that liquid
every cell largely is, all these
memory is. An easy
surrender to falling
                    asleep
on the back seat of the car.

My father's arms sliding
into the warmth between
my coat and the seat's leather
to gather my torso and limbs.
My head lolling but not swung
too hard. One arm against
his ribs. That inside hipbone—
its skinny jut—against his flat waist.
Me, curved inside his containing sweep.
Feet, boxed in patent leather,
abob in open air.
                    I wake up
wearing what I wasn't.
Awake in the place   not where I was,
my last recollection back there
where I sifted into sleep. A glass
half full of water rests on my nightstand.
Daddy must have said "Here," and lifted it
full to my lips. What, at that moment,
could I have cared for the work
of awareness? For the resurrection
memory is? My throat narrows,
grows ragged—*now I do remember*.
Grateful, I drank.

The street far below, my little-girl eyes
reached just above the window's sill.
Storeys up, in a doctor's office, I looked down
on cars and buses in single file,
on the skelter of walkers, and said
they looked like toys only because
we were high above. They'd again be big to us
once we'd walked down
the seven flights of stairs.

She's too young to be talking like that,
said the doctor in mock disapproval.
Here my mother would end
this story she liked to tell,
snugged in her notion of what
I'd been then, what I'd surely some day
become. Though just *how* young—
this story's teller far beyond asking,
she being at least as many years dead
as I'd then been alive—
I no longer know. Although
descent to ground-level,
its steady undoing, brings me closer
to the size of this bigger,
older world with every step.

REMEDY

for Nana

Above aspirin, Mercurochrome, Epsom salts,
an eye bath rested on your medicine cabinet's second shelf.
Small glass cup shaped to enclose an eye,
to wash it clean of grit. Only once did I see you lift it
to one of your eyes reddened and sore.
I closed mine. *Nonsense*, you said,
Don't be squeamish. A body heals. Sunburns
peel, scrapes scab over. Wet tea bags are good,
or wading in waves at the beach. Salt water cures
any open sore. Your broken hip not mending,
you called your surgeon—to his face—
the veterinarian he once was. Screws unmoored,
askew inside you. The chrome walker,
your dangling leg. Pain. *The only good reason*
for going to a hospital is to come home
with a baby. There's nothing a good cry
won't cure. But you never cried in front of me.

Your last surgery, exploratory,
to cut you open, sew you back up
after one hard look at the cancer's sprawl.

You look like yourself in that casket—
eyes closed, nose powdered, hands laid
across the bodice of a best dress. Not asleep,
but close. I can't take my salt-sore eyes
off your hands resting on your slack breasts.

Mom tells the story again: I'm colicky,
crying and crying after I'm born. *What this child needs—*
you tell the world—*is the sound of another heart.*
You sleep with me sleeping on your chest.

OF THE LIGHT THAT WOULD
CHANGE MY LIFE

Curtain-wavered sunlight
eased across our kitchen wall.
On our dinette table edged in chrome,
an eggplant gleamed, almost black. Reflection
blinked from the discs of my father's
frameless glasses, from the plumb bobs
of rhinestone my mother at times
hung from her ears.

I was reading the book about that backward girl
in France. Each day she wrapped
her freckled arms around a hospital's refuse
to carry its foulness off, away from the nuns
mantled like crows over their wan patients.
She climbed uphill until she could toss
the stinking bundle into a grotto nearby.
There, one day, robed in the sky's own blaze
of blue, the Madonna appeared.
Standing on bandages stiff with blood and pus,
the Virgin *spoke* to her.
Mary undid that girl's humdrum life.

I wanted to be Bernadette, *Catholic*,
to be visited by some light-steeped Lady,
her words fierce and diamond, a command
impossible for me to refuse.
                    What did I know?
Soft tick by soft tick, the clock of dusk
let luminous days leak out.
Blinded by longing, I walked
across the linoleum floor.
I flipped the light switch on.

My father taught me
to shim dimension lumber
so the level's bubble fit
between two sharp brackets, into the space
just that bubble's size. What I touch
set even.
        My mother
showed me how—in a full,
needle-spired syringe—
a bubble rose
to the top with a hard
flick of her nurse's forefinger.
Only a bead of air, it might become—
once loose in someone's veins—
a pocket of disaster. Dislodged early enough
by her jolt, its harm
could float away.
        By what
they didn't say, my parents both said
            to keep my all-too-bookish sights
set on plumb, my hand ready to ease
what's askew.
    I never wanted to be
my parents. Then they
died and I am.
Now I do.

ALONG SEVEN MILE CREEK

A light snow fell. A faint *tick tick*
as it added itself to the four foot pack.
The snowshoeing, easy. Brush bent
under the weight of our steps.
We got over obstacles
by stepping up onto them squarely.
A moment of balance.
A big step down and off.

We were able to follow the creek's path
most of the way—its water a moving stain,
a gray sough below.
Snow falling onto its surface
disappeared. The creek
ran on, unmarked.

This is marriage, I thought
as we walked high above ground,
this willingness—a union
that would be dead in less than a year.

We came to the place where a tall fir had—
years before—fallen across the creek.
A milestone of sorts,
a bridge too narrow for us to cross.
Atop its length, white leaped
over the dark current.
Seamless, of course.

On his palm   lifted toward my eyes
cough balls   he says   the balls that owls throw up.
He breaks one open   points to tiny bones
shreds of fur   gristle-threads   what the owl couldn't digest
small clots of brown scruff he's taken out of a plastic bag
this man at the door   me here alone
him talking fast all the while.

Biology labs   high school
a supplier pays him.   He can see the barn
in that field behind our house   big barn   surely owls
must roost there.   Kids opening
each one up   microscope
a worksheet to record the contents.

I lean on the door jamb   a day's work
waiting behind me   dust and dog hair
convening in corners   the week's eight loaves of bread
set to rise   a *New Yorker* story three-quarters read   laid aside.

Behind this man   across our driveway
beyond his parked pickup truck   Manning's pasture
the two mares having heard our voices
now at the fence   knowing I maybe have windfalls
for their velvety lips   maybe not. They wait.

I watch his mouth shape his soft
links of sound. The barn floor must be littered
with castings. Surely I don't mind. His hands upturned
rising toward me.   I'm barely inside
he's barely out   what can I say.

Small lives lie in his hands   white bone
a field's hidden world   its lacey chain   his voice
steady   quick   the owls his living.

In the palm of his hand   the swallowed lives
that keep broad wings beating.   How many nights
have I waited   barefoot on linoleum   everyone else
asleep   sliding open   that north window nearest the field
stark still until I can hear   owls call
back and forth across the mown hay.

He knows he has me swallowing hard
wanting so little   too much.
My voice says   I *have* to say
it's not our barn   what you want
not mine to give away.

39 BEING THE AVERAGE AGE
OF ENLIGHTENMENT, OR SO I'M TOLD

Married at that age, hard
on the heels of perfecting denial as bliss—
avoidance being my attempt
at mindful escape—
I could only wish myself
elsewhere.   Anywhere
but across the room from him that night—
the *here* where I was lying
propped up, in our bed.

He threw the alarm clock
so hard and fast at me
I could feel time's breeze graze my ear.
A gouge made where metal struck
into the carved headboard behind me
filled with grime for years.
Moving right along, I traveled
long and away into books I loved,
growing sidle-eyed, quiet,
years beyond thirty-nine.

The children grew up, moved away.
Growing too much heat for even
my stoic practice to sidestep, his fury at last
set our blear landscape ablaze.
The world lit up.
We suddenly saw only too clear
we'd been busy searing everything around us
past recognition.
What we'd turned into ash reached
far   too far beyond
the limits of our newly-gained sight.

ESTRANGEMENT

for David

Twice I've dreamt your face
up close. In the years-ago dream
I looked into your eyes and saw
only one was blue—a familiar
shade of restraint—the other
an amber so needle-clear
I couldn't look away
regardless of how I feared you. Your eyes,
even narrowed with anger,
were huge. The blue one remarkably
normal beside its uncanny partner,
both keeping a blinkless stare.

In this night's dream-roam, first I see
your hair, long and falling
in loose eddies down your neck.
Red as when we first married.
Returned to strawberry blonde,
a name too tame for its once coppery sheen.
Here is your face surrounded
by hair longer than it's ever been
in your lifetime, a length I often imagined—
when we first met—in a small ponytail,
a sweet taming at your nape.

Framed by abundance, your eyes this night
are merely *your eyes*. Small, both blue,
forgettable. This will turn out to be
a story about time and distance.
Maybe when looking into someone's eyes,

I see both at once. Maybe I gaze
a little to one side, seeing
only the half of it. So whose story is this?
Just one of our own.

FOR MY PORTRAIT PAINTER:
A REQUEST TO CONSIDER
WHAT VAN GOGH DID FOR EUGENE BLOCH

Yes, light glints from Bloch's
forehead and mustache, from the tips
of his ears and nose. His jacket
sheens with the ripeness of wheat
breeze-ridden into August.
That's not what I mean.
Look at the twilight blue surrounding
his narrow, close-cropped head.
There Van Gogh set, like gems,
fifteen stars. In a sky belonging
to neither night nor day, huge *stars*.
One the size of our sun.

This once, borrow just a bit.
Derivative is hardly a crime.
For the background, let your brushwork
loosen, let your palette find a dusk
only nudging toward black.
Then, behind my face— pale and round,
mottled, mole-stubbled, this face
traced with its own lunar lines—

behind me and on high,
add a few daubs of shine. Don't tell me
you've never seen a fullest moon
against a backdrop like that.
Even while straining to stay daylight-blue,
a sky at dusk will admit
at least a little
wild, nocturnal light.

ON THE SIDE OF MY HOUSE PAINTED BLUE

The midmorning thump
is a bolt—sharp, hard enough to quake
all the rooms.

In a sagging splatter
nine red blots string themselves
on the north side.

Impact certain, a death
for sure, but no body in sight—
no feathered clot.

Some fly south, some stay.
One flies into a blue too sudden to be
quick, wide sky.

October on the wane,
cold waxing fast. This blood-necklace
gray rain will wear away.

SOLDER

Today's laminate card says
this man is deaf, will I buy
pencils, 3 for 2 dollars, 5 for 3.
He waits at my door. *Sham* a possible
sham, but this winter day is vernal-bright,
two dollars little enough. *For shame.* No one,
for years, has come to my door peddling
so little. Decades ago, on a city bus,
a sign thrust itself at my eight-year-old eyes.
PLEASE BUY. The needles for sale
stitched themselves in pyramid steps
through a square of red foil,
the magic threader standing at apex,
silver queen, scepter-shaped. Those hands
urging the needles might have signed—
with a broken-winged flutter—
words, but were held
wordless as I. The left hand offered
those gleaming one-eyed needles,
the right held the 3 x 5 card
pleading with me to buy.

That a deaf-mute wanted
so long ago so little from me—
a child with hearing, my voice close at hand.
That my allowance, a weekly quarter,
stayed in my fist, warm solder to my grip.
A small but indelible shame.

From today's hand I pick
three silver pencils shiny as wands,
that hard flesh on their ends

the blue of this February's
boundless day. Cheap,
the erasers leave on a page
streaks of sky darker than
whatever mistakes they replace.

IN THE WORLD LYING WORLDS BELOW

To eat a morsel of the underworld's dream-food
is to die a bit. So *that's* what I've been doing
each night in my dream-life: eating
and dying, eating and dying. No.
Not so. I don't recall a dream when I actually *ate*.
One when I fried wolf meat
in a cast iron skillet, yes. And dreams where
wedding cakes lifted their tiers
like storeyed buildings
white in the sun. But none where I sat
moving food from platter to plate,
balancing forkfuls into my mouth.

But wait. Foolish me—
to be busy thinking up ways
I might remember my way out of death.
No doubt a spatter from that searing wildness
found the lips I licked. Surely I slipped
a crumb of that dream-cake under my tongue.

FROM THE VERY START

for William Stafford, whose first word was *moon*

The first word your tongue formed
for another's ear
was full as a lighted globe
traveling the dark. Maybe someone
tried to hear you saying *Mama*,
but what you uttered was so deep
at its two-fold center,
the roundness of its saying
left no room for doubt.

A room inside this sound
opened without wall or ceiling,
a passage wide as what your eyes
could take in, thin as a single
gold thread leading you through
each word-swept day. In the sky,
night or day, a glimpse of what
first shaped your breath
still sweeps my breath away—
a ready gleam that's constant
only in endless surprise.

A PLACE AT HER TABLE

for Dorothy Stafford

Tending the soup while she talks—
a little garlic, bacon, zucchini,
chicken broth, as many of her garden herbs
as the pot will hold—she adds
enough milk to make it turn
creamy, pale. *Have you been to visit*
Mt. St. Helens since it blew?
Neither have I. You and I should do that
some day. Bread into a foil packet
she crimps shut, slips into her oven's
pocketed heat. *A woman I knew*
had eighty acres there. She built
the cabin herself and set it
back in the forest so she and her husband
would have to walk a good ways
to see mountains. She claimed
they'd never take them for granted
that way. Ripe bell pepper
into a salad. Its hollow globe
red as molten glass. *I never dreamed*
that I would be the one
left alone. Me with my funny heart,
I always thought I'd be the first
to go. Cherry tomatoes from her deck's
container plants, the ones outdoing themselves
again this year. *Did I ever show you*
the note he left that day he died?
His handwriting so big, unsteady—
he must have known.
It said "And all my love."

Store-bought cookies on the counter
in their white paper package.
Easier since she cooks alone.
You know you were very much
a part of that day. Bill and I were making
a lemon pie to bring to your house for dinner.
I'm so glad I found that note. In a vase
at her bare table's shining center,
a many-sectioned, leafless branch
no bigger than her hand,
a lone ceramic wren she's tucked
near its base. On each of our placemats,
a rice paper napkin
printed with blood-bright leaves.
Bill and I kept a souvenir
from when we camped at Mt. St. Helens
years ago. I wonder if there's another
place in the world where mountains
are so separate, so much
their own selves?

IN MOTION

No. I don't know how a story works—
how tyrannies of time and space
reclaim the tailings, heap by heap,
of pretense and memory, how the narrative
seems to plead for a little violence,
a sharp edge swung against flesh,
and at the end, the story's bruise
rising to show its color.

To create character is, for me,
a process of complete mystery.
To make a *he* talk through lips of described
color and shape demands that a *she*
answer, commanding a plot
of alternative sympathies, a need
to tinker with verbs, to avoid
what simply *is*. A story's sentences
could then haggle for given proportion,
even set up housekeeping rules,
a strict division of labor.

I choose the alternative any day,
every day—a little aimless ramble
over fresh grass, my footprints
springing into disappearance behind me,
motion's sake making my way
into the poem's wild blank yonder.
Come what may.

NIGHT STORM

In last night's dark warp of heat,
lightning's jagged castoffs,
the slam of thunder, rain carousing the air,
house gutters spuming.

To think I might die with such swiftness—
a rattling plumb fall, no linger,
no languish, every going groan
blotted out.

This morning a single blue streak remains
from the chalk-art town
my grandkids and I
drew on the sidewalk.

In place of bright wavery child's play
lie a tree's tiny gold-falls—
driven down blossoms,
scattered dust of sun.

III

Flash of Pollen

A PROTHALAMION

Two swans, two deer,
two lovers. The world reflects
as couples, revealing—in its silver-quick
mirror—the deeper self
of itself in two's.

The deer's outsized ears
lift—ready to redden in pleasure.
The paired swans fledge those feathers
longing to curl themselves
skyward with joy.

What better for you to be
than two of the world's Beloveds?
Face to face each day, quicken with praise.
Reflect and be grateful.
Bow, blush, gladden.

You two are given
eyes alight enough to read—
in the mirror you each make from the other—
that couplet of oneself and oneself
your love will write.

PLATE SET BEFORE US

Flanked by blade and tines,
by the way to begin,
your white expanse waits.

Not blank, but gleaming
with our own reflection.
Plain, vitreous.

Fired in a heat so deep
color has fled every pore,
you glow with want.

Moon set on our table,
may you fill, empty,
then fill again.

AND JUSTLY SO

Accused of having no sense
of money, I take my love
by his hand out into the black
of newly minted night
and direct his eyes up
beyond a roof-peak.

Through a gap
in the spreadsheet of clouds,
my accuser and I watch
a growing balance shine.

LETTERS TOWARD THE END

I could write a hundred messages more
each ending with the same line,
the sky, that same sky for us all—
a closing called *emptiness*, *expanse*,
silence I list toward, listening.

Not complete, it carries the faint hum
of all words never said,
verbs ready to jostle through a throat,
nouns waiting to be picked
from imagination's highest limbs.

The sky. Where I was before
I was. Where I will be, after.

IT JUST SO HAPPENS TODAY I'M TIRED OF

my own voice on and on like
paint that won't peel off in one piece

guilt surrounding my mirror
in a sound-alike gleaming frame

nostalgia's bench-vise grip,
its shallow breaths all the way home

turgid rivers of human speech,
chit-chat descriptors, *I'm here*

to tell you, let me
tell you just how it is

sacrament of the over-heard,
wafer and wine of the said.

SYMPATHY FOR A FRIEND
NOT ENTIRELY BEREAVED

A friend's mother—that woman
the friend never really liked—finds the day
to die. They all do, every mother
in her ample or scant shortcomings.
The voluble, winking, all too catch-worded ones
who worry their cuticles down to the quick.
The scathe-tongued mothers, able to batter
any room into silence. Even the quiet ones
who seem to disappear just when their children
need them most, when a stepfather's fury
sends debris careening.

This friend's mother finally
does disappear. As completely as the upholstery
under those clear plastic covers she insisted
would save her family's fabric from wear.
Which is not *disappeared* at all,
but unreachable, nonetheless.

That's the trouble with death. At first
it's just an absence, and not much of one,
at that. The mother is everywhere.
In all the dresser drawers to be emptied.
In the dryer's lint, the perfumed dust
that won't quite vacuum up
from each newly vacant space. She's there
in the bottom-heavy fraction of a second it takes
her daughter to recognize
both their faces inside the mother's
wide vanity mirror.

LAST TONGUE

for Karl Marlantes

Days, maybe mere hours remain.
Your dying mother speaks only
Finnish now. Language of her youth,
left behind long ago. The words to say
dry, *mouth*, *water*, to ask
Why—if you are my son as you claim—
do you move about
in the body of my father, why?
all this spoken in the clack and clang
of her mother tongue. Time throws open
a window, a young world
pours back in. Her tattered breathing
sucks at its air.

WIDOWS

In cards, it's an extra hand
dealt to the table. In printing,
a last line carried over
to hover alone at the top
of a next page. Among what's alive,
it's a woman whose husband
isn't, that same woman
not married again.

Forming a man's counterpart
takes a mere two letters more.
But wait. A *dealer* deals. A *printer* prints.
How can a he whose wife is dead
be called *widower*, as if *he's* the one
making a woman whose husband
is gone? Impossible. Unless
he must die a little too.

The widower deals
cards to her empty space
at their table, playing both her hand
and his own. He carries along
some final words from her
to start the blank page staring at him
each day. At last, *he's* taken
another's name—the one
that would have belonged to his wife,
had she survived him.

ONE WORK OF THIS EARTH

All night long, in a season of heat,
it gives off warmth, drinks in coolness.
Beginning at daybreak, it gathers sun
and releases the cold it's stored.
In winter, it freezes
only so far, then stops.

Its work is the great *evening-out*,
hoarding what's needed,
then giving away what's not.

Those who creep, who burrow—
mole pushing the star of its nose
through dirt, half grown vole
under the leaf-mold litter,
lizard in the rimrock cranny—

all low-lying creatures,
earth lets them huddle close.

AN ATLAS OF TASTE

First and quick, its tip darts to test
the world for sugar—oblivious to all else.
The tongue senses sweet,
and only sweet, at its apex.
Leaves the rest to those parts of itself
lagging behind.

Salt it detects on both flanks, an inch or so
to the rear. Sour it sidelines to the back
even farther, right and left.

Oh, easy enough a tongue can say
candied, briny, squinch.
But only across its thick base—
nearest that lout, the throat—
will the tongue recognize what's hardest
to swallow. There's plenty of time, too much
time to say what's bitter.

PAYING ATTENTION

for my friend Carlos, who says you can carry the moon
by catching its reflection in a bucket of water

This heavy bucket's become
too light. The moon's gone
and disappeared when I wasn't looking.
She didn't say a word. She must have cut me off
days ago, quiet-like,
in one of her classic slow fades
until the bucket was swinging easy as I walked,
my arm a little giddy from lack.

I miss the heft of her hard lesson
in gravity. I want her back. Let the bail
cut welts into my palm.
Let my fingers ache and stiffen.
I want the moon,
fat as ocean, crusted with sky-salts—
every ounce she can muster.
I won't complain again.

May my legs buckle. May I be forced
to shift the weight from hand to hand.
I can stop every so often.
Set the bucket down on a somewhat
level spot. Catch my breath, take a look.

The water's surface stills. Little ripples
heal themselves, settle back into their bigger,
flatter self. Surrounded by a galvanized rim,
the moon's splayed face
seems to stare back at me again.

I lean closer.
What is she saying?
Only something looking far too much
like my own long-dead mother
rises to answer me.

EARLY IN THE OCEAN'S PRESENT LIFE, YOU APPEAR

What can empty seawater from the clouds?
Not your tongue insisting on only
sweetness in rain—but the rain itself,
finding its way. Along street gutters, through
sewer pipes tall enough for upright walking.
Down into pine duff, scree, the mud
lining a gully. Overland, underground,
blindly melding into rivulets
roaming their way to streams streaking
into rivers rovering on to a sea-mouth
glimmered and slicked with salt.

What empties from clouds is an ocean
before it knows who it is—too fresh
to have come of age. Close your umbrella,
lift your face. A sheer tide falls.

CAPITAL

for Salem, Oregon

River-carved city, green with leaf-light,
in you our civil law is born.
Beneath your rotunda that shoulders the sky, *accord*
calls us to set conflict aside.

Salem, we're speaking *Peace* each time
we say your name.
Salaam, shalom. At your site, our mapmakers place
a star's steady shine.

REMEMBERING MY COPY OF *A Glass Face in the Rain* WAS LONG AGO BORROWED AND NEVER RETURNED

What people borrow late in a day
morning often forgets—like a book
with a title so transparent
every eye watches from its cover.
How could a lender ever expect
to have such a thing returned?
What you might lend in an offhand moment—
not pausing to open its first pages
and write a line of ownership there—
is off and running on its own, unchaperoned.
What a boon, in the midst of such
passing exchanges, to be that former owner,
the one feeling a bit light-headed,
your arms suddenly weightless, rising.
You're left here holding *nothing*,
exactly what you once owned.

WHY THE AGING POET CONTINUES TO WRITE

At a coneflower's seed-making center,
hundreds of tiny dark florets—
each stiff and sharp—
take turns oozing
their flashes of pollen.
A flagrant
bee-stopping show.

Making a bright circle,
the outermost spiky blossoms
open first to then fade.
Shrinking day by day,
the ring of yellow flame
moves inward.
That heart—what's at
the flower's very core—
blazes last.

AIRBORNE

Our plane, still on tarmac,
gains speed. Raindrops
splay into pinpoint beads,
then skitter across
the oval of window glass.

A shudder of derring-do,
and we're suddenly
aloft. Within a mere
held breath or two,
we're in clouds far above
the city of my birth and youth.

Roof, bridge, tree
flatten beneath these wings.
No turning back. Already
I come from a place
with a mother tongue
arcane, melodic.
From the *where* named *else,*
I become the exotic.

IV

Shimmer and Drone

BEGINNING WITH 'AND'

Golkanda Fort, Hyderabad, India

Five days into India,
and finally a sight of India's moon.
Huge silver crescent with Venus below,
these two heavenly creatures
above the silhouetted walls
of an ancient Sultan's fortress city.
Moon and evening star.
The same moon, same star
that rise—wherever I live—to beckon
darkness down and deeper.

All this life I've seen the crescent moon
as parenthesis—
left or right, a curl of light
to hold something in,
to mark its end. But here the crescent
is a resting bowl, an outstretched hand
cupped to hold its own light,
slimmest fingers
curving silver into the dark.

India's moon is upturned,
filling with late dusk's violet-blue.
It's a calligrapher's single stroke
for *and*, that curving sweep
from the Arabic pen—
the word that's written before all others,
symbol that beckons us
to listen. A story begins with *And*.
Because it has never
ended, will never have to end.

THE WORLD BEGINS THIS EVERY INSTANT

The Lakshmi Temple, Mumbai, India

Naked except for white dhoti,
sacred thread, and the vermilion seared
between his brows, the priest sits
cross-legged on the raised altar. From our clamor
of lifted hands, he scoops flowers,
sweetmeats, and plates of fruit
to stuff around Lakshmi's gilded likeness.
Then dishes them, once they're blessed,
back to each giver, kind for kind.
Any coconut to the coconut-giver,
some sweets—*any* sweets—
to the giver of sweets.

At this temple of the goddess
whose flower is the lotus, our offerings
are taken and then returned,
but never returned exact.
Like is as close
as the Brahman priest comes
to keeping strict accounts.

I offer a pink lotus,
heavy in its full, star-rayed bloom.
Barely open, its pale bud
returns to my hand.

EXHALATION

for Priya Adarkar

This alphabet, you say,
is spoken in the order
its sounds come from the body.
First the vowels, their ripeness
clustered low in your throat, Priya,
whose own name means
she who speaks sweetly—
each liquid sound
a perfect bubble of voice
risen into my hearing.

Then gutturals, palatals,
dentals, labials rising
into and out of the mouth's
dark cave. An alphabet
that follows the path of breath
leaving the body. Discreet sounds
that combine and shift and recombine
to form the words of your
ancient tongue. Sanskrit—
language whose own epithet is
tongue of the gods.

Sound itself, and the small cup
of ear in which to gather
its nectar: these are gifts divine
from Brahma. I listen as you breathe in
the scent, the very air of this world.
Then breathe it out as song.
A wordful, sweet singing.

WHITE NOISE, YELLOW DUST

The Ganesh Temple, Mumbai, India

Eye-level on either side. Flower chains
dozens deep, row after row.
Garland vendors outside Ganesh's shrine
that's domed in a gold rich as any hive.
Needle-pierced lumps of jasmine, hibiscus,
marigold, rose—perfume strung
on coarse thread. In stall after stall
after stall, right and left.

I pass between two walls of the shorn,
bruised, already browning. Weight of dust,
and at each hanging garland, the bees. Yellow,
sooty, dun, large and small,
they burrow, dart. *Bees.*

Beggars swarm, touching my clothes,
my pale arms, hands. *Madam, Madam.*
Wisps of fingertips pluck, tug.
Madam, please, Madam. Palms cupped.
Begging bowls thrust under my sidling eyes.
Their gazes bold, brows rising.
Five, six deep—moving only when
I try to. They dart then hover. *Madam.*

My pathway lined with sotted shimmer, drone.
Each garland pushed at my face to *buy, buy*
is a flower-wick dripping temple bees.
Madam, only 7 Rupees.   Hovering smother.

Thick clamor, tunnel of quick
prickle-touch. *Wait Madam, please.*
Their thrum a muffle filling my ears—
this hum shutting nothing out—
no way to appease.

THE TABLA PLAYER

From his wrist's smooth underside,
this moan. His fingers and palm
arched back like a bird's alerted head, he slides
the inside of his wrist across the larger,
rounder female of his two drums, so the tabla
calls out with a woman's cry—
short swoop of desire.

On this drum skin stretched
achingly taut, his fingertips find fire's staccato,
its rapid drops.
Lengths of finger make
clear needle-slaps.

Then again, with his underwrist's thin skin—
that pulse-point where his blood pounds
so strongly another can count its beats—
he calls forth her groan.
His own heartbeat presses
the heart of his drum.

Birdcall like a fast-ticking clock
tells the time when cows herded home
fill the air with a golden film.
Such a quick song emits the world—
note by duple note, this *ever-and-all*
propelled from a bird's throat.

6 PM, and plopped from birdsong,
the sun sits down behind the Deccan plain.
Sky at its horizon tries out
the underside of bougainvillea-flush
spilling over the rim and into night.

Each scrap, midge, and peak is plinked
into existence by this late-day singsong.
A *ping, ping, ping* for each mote
raised to make *the cowdust hour*.

WORSHIP REQUIRES YOU TO JOLT
THE GOD AWAKE

A second ago, his body—
replete with sets of arms, with lotus navel—
reclined on the coils of a snake
whose thousand heads flared above him,
protecting his sleep with a hood of cobra shade.
Across his dream, like ten jewels
strung on a spun-gold thread,
his avatars arrayed themselves.
Fish, tortoise, lion and boar,
a boy licking blue-skinned, buttery hands.

Small wonder that Vishnu's attention to your prayer
is brief. Your offer of sweetmeats, sandalwood,
marigold garland, camphor and anointing oil
are mere amends for what
you've made him leave behind—
yours being small consolations
for his loss of sleep. At the close of his eyes,
he breeds carapace, mane, snout, fins. Ever young,
he divides himself into as many languorous,
stiff-membered Lords as the countless
girls crazing for him.

A great bee drones the air,
beats its wings so fast
they are the bow drawn
above the stringed hole
of this tremolo violin—

bee whose hunger-note
soars and rolls, grows long
and then is broken short
to roam longer once more,

the bee sipping yellow at the bowl
of your mouth's open poem,
the one whose sole home
is the honeycomb in your ear's
chambered cove.

OF THE HEAT THAT BROODS THIS WORLD

Elephanta Caves, off the shore of Mumbai

Immense three-headed stone Shiva
deep inside this sea-ringed cave—
you whose ardor creates
the heat that creates this world,
that destroys all worlds—nothing
can distract you from your meditations.

Not earthquake.
Not the ancient Portuguese marauders
who came swinging stone-crumbling hammers.
Not the noisy tourists
whose cave-garb includes
sunglasses and caps with brims
turned backward to shade their napes.
Nothing disturbs you, Meditating Shiva.

Not even the three white flowers
a devotee places as high as her fingers
can reach—an offering she sets
on the stone necklace
carved to curve above your collarbone.
The sole flames in this hushed dim,
not even these blooms open your eyes.
Thick-petaled, fragrant,
far from their overhead home.
Not even such flesh-fallen stars.

AS FOR THE APPEAL OF A CERTAIN
AVATAR'S SWEET, ANDROGYNOUS LOOKS

He grew up on a butter so white and frothy
it fills a bowl with its cloud.
Such mounds of confection arise
from celestial cows as slender-faced and flanked
as deer with their sloe-cast eyes.

Milk can be so sweet its globules of fat
are white, not yellow, their traces on his fingertips
a mere sheen. His own milkless breasts preside
above a nipped waist. Inside his mouth rimmed with butter,
the whole universe resides.

Krishna's skin is enough blue to call him
Obscure One. That blue can grow deep enough
to divide him into as many sleepless nights
as the number of women who long to suckle him, bed him,
O Black One, Dark One, divine.

INDIAN MINIATURES

See the brush of creation pay no attention to perspective—
every stroke of story flush with your eye.

•

Escaping Jyaistha, month
of most sun, an elephant stands
in leaf-shade. With the heat enough
to blunt ancient hate,
a tiger sleeps in the double shade
the elephant's belly provides.

•

With pronged tongue, a cobra
reaches to sip at the cup
girlhood extends from her window.
The curtain that covers
the entry below
flares to let us see
her door is locked.

•

Through thunder clouds
as blue as Krishna's thumb
pressing into Radha's nipple,
gold-rope lightning
unfurls.

•

A lake props itself sideways—
wall of gray water,
it lets us peer
into the yellow heart
of each lotus bloom's
vermilion burst.

EVAPORATION

For a last time, my hair dries
in India's air—releasing, drop
by minute drop, Mumbai water,
my scalp and neck warming
with each second gone.

In yesterday's minutes I watched
a granite woman's hands—her face
broken away centuries ago—squeeze water
from the thick rope of just-washed hair
falling along the carved crevice
between her chest and upper arm.

A wrapping of stone-film over stone,
her sari still drips from her bath,
that fabric a second skin so silky sheer
it disappears—except at its hem—
against her breast-mounded,
hip-canted form.

Hair drying, it's mere
hours until my departure, my meltable,
shifting skin already too warm.
I'm as good as gone. From that statue whose eyes
I cannot even try to meet,
time drops, rises from her so slowly
it doesn't. If I held myself
still for a lifetime,
I could not see how still
she holds onto what remains.

TRANSPORTED

Light in the sky, at my eye's
rim. Flick of recognition.
An airplane, I think,
where I'll soon be. Not so.
It's the moon, sliver of crescent
upturned. Shallow bowl
floating in thick dusk,
India's moon on my last
Mumbai night.

For an instant I see
the creature willing
to take me in its silver belly,
lift me from one world
into another. A slightest
blink, then I see
the new moon.
For once, twice,
I am right.

V

A Same Sky

Beginning at the hem, silk stitches flow into waves
of river and ocean. Then the four summits
loft themselves, steeply sloped and snow-topped—
those cardinal directions of land.
Above and above is sky, sewn plumes
of cloud, expanse enough to hold
a dragon's metallic light.
On each robe of the emperor,
of his princely and imperial families,
the embroidered universe rises.

Still, such splendid stitching
is nothing more than mere shell
without its center, a man,
his body the axis for all matter,
his godly head above the collar's
gate of heaven. How regal
each family member. How eye-weary
the royal embroiderer.

That seamstress turns
from her work. She places within a lidded basket
the silk-tailed needle, silver
fingerling
that dipped and rose with each stitch of world.
Most simple of tools, her needle returns
to source and substance,
back to the earth-making colors.
It rests with a bundle of floss—thin swimmer,
its glint adrift in the twisting
eddy of blue.

THE SILENCE AFTER

for Carla, in Ermoupolis

Four o'clock and nothing moves
in this house on an island's hill
but the fine sift of plaster
fallen on spiral stairs.

Each stairstep bears the print
of the one who climbed it,
sole and toes exactly marked
where they lifted dust from paint.

The woman taking a nap upstairs
married the husband who's left her
because of his silence. She believed
his brooding beauty held

nothing less than a poet's soul.
Now he's gone, and she tells again
the story of betrayal.
Empty, she says, silent and cold.

Decades of marriage swept away
in his letter of four lines,
its paper fingered to a soft cloth.
She folds and unfolds that page

in her mind as she climbs
the city's stair-stepped streets,
then the staircase that rises
in her high-ceilinged house.

Once she believed his silence
would break in waves against
her love, words spilling
like foam from its source.

She tells this story into the sweep
of sea, against the sun's glare,
across a taverna's table spread
with empty bottles, half-empty plates.

Having filled the morning
with how he sailed these waters
island to island, fearless
in the worst of storm or calm,

how their sons grew brown-skinned
and salt-bleached on rocky shores,
her voice stills. Four lines,
not a word more. She turns away

from the sea's hammered blue,
its rushing noise. She climbs
the city's white tiers, reaching
that house where winding stairs

rise and rise. Shoes in hand,
she places one foot, then another
onto the dusty wood, turning toward
the wordless sleep of afternoon.

WHERE YOU BEGAN YOUR SINGING

for Olga Broumas, born on the island of Syros

Wild capers ooze their green
from doorstep crevices,
in bloom as soon as leaves unfurl.
Priced by the quarter-kilo, mounds
of their salt-dried buds swell from bins
outside the markets edging cobbled streets.
Matrons in dark, belted dresses—
might they remember you as a child?—
chafe at the price of each eggplant, each egg.

I walk these sloping streets.
All of this summer's month—for a full array
of the moon's pregnant shapes—
I've lived on your native Syros,
island of your birth. I've climbed, swam,
brooded. I've taken the sun,
escaped it in afternoon's reeling heat.

Marble stairs cut into inclines—crumbling,
steep. In the Church of the Metamorphosis, an old woman
rises again and again to light a taper. Old one
loose in confusion and neglect, she kisses
an icon's second skin of glass—her unwashed body
so ripe with its own fumes
curls of incense stand to one side
each time she moves.

On your island's west shore, in coarse sand,
mothers and daughters, mamas and pampered sons
wade the wave-line—the sea's recent cargo of tar

blotching their feet with the black, adhesive
work of Hades, Lord of the Dark.

Homer sang of your island's peace.
Gentle Syros, apart from war.
Filled with olive trees, plots of onion and garlic,
the curl of its grapevines dusted by Cycladic light.
A life so sweet, said Homer, old men
didn't fear death. A prick of silver or gold—
arrows from the Moon or Sun's quiver—
took them without pain. Suffering
was for the keening women left behind,
waiting years before they unearthed
a husband's bones to be washed in wine.

I met the man who still dyes widow's clothes.
He lives on Ano Syros, your island's highest hill.
For a few drachmas, he'll steep
a grieving woman's dresses in his huge pot
of inky broth. Why buy new, he tells the widows,
when what you already have will do?
Of the old women, Homer did not sing.

At an abandoned pier, where the Aegean
meets a bit of steepest shore, townsfolk
swim and sun. The old maid Evangelia—
thick glasses, ratted hair, heavy middle
snugged into a bathing suit's sheen—
breaks into song. Her lyrics come from Seferis' lines.
Doves fly inside the refrain.
They rise from the plaka's stone pavement,
flying from cote to cote in the island cliffs.

Everywhere, they lap the air with lines from Elytis,
with Sappho's scraps of song—
tropes for a violet-crowned woman,
dill sprigs twining her neck.
Greek doves zigzag the air in waves,
their wings soughing poems
starting with *O* for *ocean,*
beginning with *O* for you.

THE VILLAGE DYER MAKES WIDOW'S WEEDS

With my wooden paddle, I stir and stir,
sliding her skirts, blouses, her dress—
its roses vined across a silky sheen—
into my tub of inky soup. No need,
I told this newly widowed one,
to spend precious drachmas
on a dressmaker's goods. What *was*
can become in the time of a breath
what has to be. She'll see.

Now each thread sucks at the dye
with a withered tongue. Each garment
becomes the shade created
to swallow light—a night that will
in its wearing surround
the new moon of her separate flesh.

AUBADE

A canary, its feathers
a gash of coral,
rolls its pinwheel of sound
over heaps of okra,
eggplant, leeks. It wends
its song between fly-pestered
slabs of hanging meat,
spending itself without hesitation,
without pause to breathe,

like the one who loans
it color, she who will
tonight loom full
on the Aegean horizon,
poised—in her wild
throb of borrowed heat—
to let, to leave, to trill
rosy blood across a dark sea.

Onto this island halved by patriots,
rain refuses to fall.
Years of drought. Then an hour's lightning.
Fire shrieks up mountainsides,
blaze harrows from cedar to pine.

Not an olive tree, an oleander,
nothing left. What can grow
from such blistered stone, such drifting ash?

Wild poppies. Their crimson silk floods
across boundary, claiming
the *all* of blackened ground.
Through eras of Turk on Greek,
Greek at Turk,
kindred warring kin,
the seeds have endured.

Gorge, slope, ledge,
the whole island pulses
with a single blood, this red of reds—
earth's deep heart finding
its way into bloom.

FROM THE WHOLLY HORIZONTAL

Felled and limb-trimmed
long enough ago to be sun and rain-bleached,
a pile of cottonwood trunks
lies off the side of an Anatolian road.
No bark, not even the saw's rawness remains.
Mere logs now,
lengths ready to be lumber.

Yet from them, green prongs sprout
straight up, bursting
with pennants of cottonwood leaves.

Nurse log—now I recall
those huge, fallen, crumbling firs
of an Oregon rainforest sending up
green fire. Tiny trees
chartreuse in their birth.

No sex. No bees.
Even seedless, the world
yearns itself alive.

LAST NIGHT, WHEN SHE SEEMED ASLEEP

A poppy, she saw her red
blotted up by night, her waxy center-stains
swallowed into dark. Her black
grew deeper. Her sheen fled.
The fur on her limbs
prickled with blindness.

She scoffed at the portulaca
closing its ruffled skirts at dusk.
She swooned from the thick perfume
of a moonflower
disrobing for midnight's eyes.
She would not open wider,
would not close herself tight.

Little Bride, they name her
in Anadolu—a crenelated silk
her one true skin.
An hour before the dawn,
she shivers into that breeze
the oncoming sun lets loose—
its sudden clumsy touch
her new groom.

AT A WISHING-SPRING ON A TURKISH
MOUNTAINSIDE MILES ABOVE THE BLACK SEA

for Ken

Stop to see whatnot tied
to trees and bushes, a ragged clutter.
In its midst, water emerges
from rock. Stare at that thin, falling stream—
its syllables a sound
only an ear drawn close could hear.
A creek below takes this spring's quiet
into its clatter, the creek then taken
into a river's plunging noise
farther down.

Be wearing what's frayed or tattered.
Tear off a thread, a scrap.
Or the bit of string forgotten in your pocket. Use that.
Tie whatever you can to an empty twig
leaning near the spring.
Then cup your hands under the flow, bow to drink.

Far below, another salty throat
swallows the sweet water
a river gives up, at last.
Be ocean-lucky. Make your wish.

WHY, OF RENOIR'S WORKS, HIS FLORAL
BOUQUETS INTEREST ME THE LEAST

A bather's breasts, belly-roll, thighs,
the languid flow of her towel.
A young girl's wisps of hair
flown from her flat straw hat—
that skimmer, its planetary gleam.
A stippled crockery jug, the table's cloth
dusted with yellow smudge, a sleeve's tuck
and ruche. They're oozing nectar, one and all.

Whatever his eyes could hold.
However it left his brush's tip.
Every swell or dimple of flesh and weave,
each whatnot, each bijou he laid on the canvas
emerges
        fully in bloom.

SET TO RISE

Moon-teeth some bakers in France
call the crescent rolls they make—
curls of yeast dough they slide
into ready heat. Enough
on a barely-lipped baking sheet
to bite across a clear, lack-a-daisy
summer night, scattering
tooth marks on the next morning's
cast-over sky. Golden tusks
inside the oven's pocket of sun,
layer by flaky layer, they rise.

A *moon-tooth*? Mais non.
These bakers fashion the moon's
winter breath, her buttery breast,
the sway of her pregnant belly.
They only begin to credit the ways
they get her right: a buttock's
curve at the top of one thigh,
a horn that might prick—
if she were to sprout horns—
through her mat of verdigris hair,
those pale crescents risen upon
each of her fingernails.

AS NOTED IN MUSEUMS OF NOTE

Egyptians had flat, protracted feet.
They preferred to stand and sit
entirely in profile.

People take turns
to take their pictures of a picture
in which Van Gogh
depicts himself.

If a Venus' marble proportions
epitomize Greek perfection,
they're accorded
a separate vaulted hall. Being
Love so precisely
can get lonely.

As others step aside
to avoid being in the family photo
she's taking in front of the cuneiform tablets,
a woman can say her *Gracias* in all
understandable tongues.

Slowly circling, packed five and six deep,
each with a camera in hand,
the fans of a reclining hermaphrodite
queue up for the chance to get
those breasts and penis included inside
a single frame.

From his shoulders, like wings,
a wooden Bodhisattva extends

five hundred pairs of arms.
Thousand-handed compassion.
A thousand times five
gold-brushed fingertips
reach out with their merciful gleam.

Talking on her cell phone,
a fashionista can pass by—without a glance—
the case of masterpiece mirrors and combs.

Highlights tell a story.
Every subject of a famous
European portrait painter
turns out to be
heliotropic.

Even when rendered in stone,
arms are fragile,
a finger
more so.

HOW FRIDA KAHLO SPEAKS OF COLOR

I know of a bruja who wants to die.
Old as she is—almost one hundred—
she cannot until she passes on
the lonely art of her poison.
She steps out of a creek,
hand-in-hand with a young girl.
Oak leaves crackle and stir
as the two walk, the tannin-water—
its yellow *the color of sickness and fear,*
part of the sun and of joy—
dripping from their clinging skirts.

In early dawn a curandera
dreams of a mountain lion.
As she stands on a low bridge
spanning a dry river's tumble of rocks,
the cat leaps in effortless, glittering arcs,
then lies in the empty streambed below her.
Unafraid, she sees its face is human —
pale, imploring. The eyes fixed on hers
are cobalt blue. *Electric and pure.*

Another woman steps from a sidewalk
into a street of a great city.
Cars drive by her, pausing only
for the red of a traffic light.
Lifting her dress, she squats.
With her matted hair thrown forward,
she looks between her legs
to watch the stream—
brilliant, chartreuse in the sun.
Ghosts wear clothes of this hue.

Look at me. Look at my hands.
For this occasion I painted—
in *old blood of the prickly pear,*
most alive and ancient of colors—
all but the half-moon
of each fingernail.
Ten pale moons
shine in ten red skies.
Witch, angel, outcast—
they are the ones
whose portraits I paint.
These sisters haunt,
they rise from my hands.

THE CAVE-PAINTER'S MANIFESTO

The night sky pocked with light
can pine and fend for itself.
Let water shift, moaning
on its own. Clouds
will have to hie themselves along
with no notice from me.
I come here having
sloughed off the upper world's
tight skin. I swear,
no trees, no mountains,
never a river or star. I paint
only the stag, aurock, and ibex
to low from this rocky wall—
their vulvas, stiff members.
I add, one atop another,
only our blooded kin,
those born from a mother's
oozing cave.

Bison, huge cousin,
I dip into my paint dish
to widen your eye. Black I took
from a lightning-seared trunk.
Red from a powder of bloodshot stone.
Now   I make your eye wild,
light-rimmed. My grease lamp glimmers.
You jitter   I startle.   This flame
I carried here from sun-struck day
quickens your haunches.
Your withers tremble.
Take your sisters and brothers
dust-roiling   deeper.
Go ahead   lead the way
plunge your herd down.

OUT OF SEASON

April. A Latina on one of California's
countless Mendocino Avenues
glides with swollen shopping bags
slung from her hands.
A watermelon's waxy globe
floats atop her head.

How simply she carries
another hemisphere's green heat
balanced on her crown.

PLAYA PUBLICO, THE SEA OF CORTEZ

The lips her mama's sure
no boy has touched
burn with juice, with salt,
while waves ride her waist, breast, waist,
their cool surprise waking her nipples
under the bathing suit's film.

Standing in an August sea, swaying,
the girl eats a mango.
In one hand, strips of cinnabar skin,
in the other a swell of rose-gold meat,
her teeth and tongue pulling bits of flesh
from the seed's coarse fur
until juice veins her throat again,
and she lifts another handful
of sea to her skin.

Behind her, children roll
in a slurry of waves and sand.
An old woman, slippers shuffling,
steps into the water's feathered edge.
The girl turns back to shore, the taste
of mango and sea rough on her lips—
sated by this sweet and salt,
content with this public joy.

A COLONIAL TRANSLATION

Of the nine Mayan words for 'blue' that Spaniards included
in the Porrua Spanish-Mayan comprehensive dictionary,
six they left untranslated.

Imagine—under air
too rarefied for easy breath—
that blue of a lake at dawn suddenly
gone. Or three wide
(dusky and bluer and bright)
swaths of twilight sky, lost.
Or a reclusive bird's flash
of gorget, no more. That's five
forced toward the Underworld's
silencing depth.

And the blue-black shadow
made when certain grasses lean over
other grass, darkness
bleeding the yellow light
out of green blades?

Imagine such shade gone too.
Pointed toward its death,
the withering Mayan tongue
carried these six along—over,
then under the now duller earth's
newly rounded edge.

Returned from night, the sky
looks back at our city with newly
blue eyes. What it saw on the other side
of this world while most of us slept
would have kept us from sleep
had we been looking too. Enemy rockets
blew up the approximate spot
from which rockets had screeched toward them
the day before. Tit for tat, on and on, there,
in their daytime while most of us slept.
A notch in the aimer's weapon. A crater
in the target's terrain. Cities, villages erupt
with ulcers of crumbled concrete,
broken stone. We watch on TV.

The only sound here is tire on asphalt
a block away, a breeze through the top
of this neighborhood's tallest trees.
The only rubble is blossoms fallen
in a moist heap under the hibiscus.
Those few pollen-laden bees
too old, too tattered to fly away,
are the only casualties in sight. Left from night
is what the sky saw below itself
while we slept. The heavens that covered—
just hours ago—another half of the world with blue.
The same sky for us all.

Barrow of rubble. Burial mound
of blown-apart concrete, broken stone
where a bomb struck an hour ago.
In that pile of debris, a mother digs.
With bleeding hands she pulls
at chunks of her family home—
pieces of wall, doorway, roof—
to find the body

this war buried. To pry him
from a bomb-made, makeshift grave.
To wash his limbs with rose water
and wind him in a clean, white cloth.
To keen over the pine coffin
adorned with only that name
she gave him at his birth.
To bury her child
again, in spade-broken earth.

SO SPIRIT WILL LIVE IN OUR MIDST

for the Pueblo people

Because stars are washed
out of the night by light
we make too cheap.

Because prayers grow too heavy to rise.

Because our world soaks the Earth
with blood—soldier-blood,
the blood of broken treaties,
broken forests,
broken-down stream banks,
the blood of poisons unwilling
to break down.

You be who you have always been,
the sons of Father Sun.
Rekindle our world each dawn.

I'll be who I've learned to be,
one of the countless offspring of air,
daughter to what we breathe.
Ordinary, singing my workaday songs.
Blood kin to the sky warming
in sunlight, cooling under
a clan of stars.

VI

Half Heaven

How much longer can she go on
with her mouth full of this fire,
what she should have passed on
to someone else long ago?
If, at the very start, she'd kissed
that boy, given him this heat,
she'd have been a swan. White.
A stillness arching from the lake—
motionless even in motion,
her webbed feet pulling at water
below the threshold of sight.

A thousand thousand times
she could have spoken out,
opened her mouth to tell of what
lay behind every word she said.
Then, merely scorched here and there,
she could have rolled in the dust.
Been a she-dog mottled by burns,
a lizard blistered and crinkle-skinned,
a dusky cat with only one
white foot to lick.

Too late. Smoldering to the bone,
she turns this way and that,
seeking the air
that will breathe her to flames.
She's the night with no day
to follow. Given in,
she swallows all color.
She *is* a swan, seared to black.
Wind worries her wings.

THE MOON IN HER PHASES

The moon is a rabbit living inside a bottle high in the sky,
her white fur shining through the bottle's thick glass bottom.

At the start—belly sucked in—
she lies on her side,
back pressed against the bottle's curve,
hind legs and long ears
stretched out to make
a thin curl. But she can't abide
being that artful for long.

For days, she eats and drinks
what she wants.
Her body eases, slumping
wide. Her belly spreads,
rolls off to the side,
filling that bottle.

Other days, hungry and dwindling,
she's more like the rest of us
here, on the downhill slope—
making do
with less and less until
she disappears.

•

Old wives swear that flax
will bleach to silver-white
if laid in the light of a moon.
So a ship is moved on churning salt
by sails made with goods
borrowed from the sun.

•

Maybe you've seen her,
the one in a corner, too old
to marry. Day after day
to earn her keep, she pumps pumps
a treadle, spinning the tax
of virgin's wool
due from each house.

•

A king orders his tablecloth
spun with pale fibers
gathered from crumbled rock.
At banquet his guests watch in thrall
as he flings it stained
into the fire. Then plucks it out
burned clean again.

•

Bless the bridegroom, bless
his clumsy groomsmen who must
make cloth for the bride's gown.
At night the groom undoes each day's
careless work, then makes it anew.
She is wed in the faultless
weave of his hands.

•

Locked in a story's ordeal,
what can a maiden do but obey?
She must gather and spin
stinging nettles. Her fingers, palms
swell to a fullness of roses
pricked into bloom.

•

St. Catherine's body tears apart
on the spokes of a great, spinning wheel.
Faster and faster—slowly it whirls her
out of flesh and bone
into the glowing
thread of her passion.

•

The first Fate, spindle in hand,
makes an umbilical cord.
The second opens her arms
to give it length.
With silver scissor the third Fate
cuts a newborn loose,
spins her into this world.

THE MOON REVEALS HOW
CERTAIN COATS GET THEIR GLEAM

I ride the sky's black sea
in a copper boat—stowing
my burnished vessel
with voles and packrats,
crows, magpies and cranes.
Voyaging earthward far enough
to touch river, lake, pond,
I linger on watery skin,
letting creatures go wherever my light
laps a silver shoreline.

Of course, I give them names—
Grayburr, Whiteflash—telling them
to scat, go make your eggs and sperm.
Burrow, squawk, flap, copy
a little talk. The traces of metal
that smeared into your feathers and fur
while you were riding in my boat
won't rub off.

At my behest, you fell to earth
held tight in copper's craft.
Every bit of sun's heat will travel
your length, soaking in—
hoard it for the cold.
Tying sky to ground
with its tinsel streak,
each bolt of lightning
will make you shine.

NOTIONS

In ancient lands where freight
was transported by wheel,
people knew for sure
the sun rode across heaven's blue way
in his 18 karat chariot.

Places where goods were moved by barge,
it was obvious: folks figured the sun
was carried aboard a sky-boat,
lolling on its wide deck.

And those places where people
toted things themselves, on foot?
In such spots, the sun needed something
to guide him as he loped along—
a rope up there, on high,
strung from dawn to dusk.
Any mortal could take the time
to watch the sun move—his blazing right hand
skimming the line that kept him
walking on course.

Now—inside an aircraft's shining belly—
people far above us   walk, chat, nap
and snack while they *themselves* fly through the sky.
The sun stands still. We seldom look up.

FOUR OF THE STARGAZERS

1

The fish is one of the sea's bottom-dwellers,
spiny, bone-clad,
its eyes having ages ago
floated to the top of its head.

2

A dose of viscous perfume, the flower
is an Asiatic lily,
its eye-spots, reddened with pollen,
lifted toward our star, the sun.

3

Belonging to the group called *sky-scrapers*,
the sail is that smallest triangle
hoisted above
a moon-sail's little square.

4

In other circles, a stargazer's the one
who's looked up and away
enough too often
to be looked down on.
Amateur, dreamer, a poet
most likely. Or someone who's read
far too many poems.
A misfit vainly looking to
constellate the earth.

5

One extra. That not-too-distant cousin,
the *stargazey*, namely a pastry made
from pilchards and leeks,
an onion-and-whole-fish pie.
The head of each pilchard is left
sticking out of the crust—
a head gone crisp and wrinkly

from gazing up too long
into all that heat,
open-eyed.

GUISE

To see through the eyes of a god, wear that god's mask.

Your hair becomes a hank
taken from a river animal's pelt.
Your face is carved from that tree
whose thick trunk grew near your home,
wood-grain telling the seasonal story
of rain and sun. A pronged moon,
a star, one zigzag of lightning
paint themselves onto each cheek.

From the opening made for your mouth—
its rim swollen, stained berry-red—
you hear your voice
speak words of a language
you've dreamed you'd one day know.
From behind the holes for seeing,
your trying-hard-not-to-act-ordinary
eyes peer through.

You see people hand-and-kneeing
their way backward, away
from your disfavor. Upright,
they sway themselves into dance steps
only frenzy could count and recall.
On, on, and on. You're stuck.
They know enough not to turn
their backs to your wooden face.

ROSE WHITE TELLS HER STORY

Father's yard of blanched grass
once ended in a rose hedge
keeping at bay dark thickets
of poplars and red-berried yews.
Croon, croon, I sang leafy lullabies
to those trees. Deer bedded down
in shade their branches cast.
Daring to browse the edge
of father's mown plot, they ate
the blown roses. Fey doe,
flare-eyed buck, they allowed
my hand within inches
of their twitching ears.

Just before I was born,
Father cleared the plot surrounding
his limestone house and planted
that hedge of white briar rose.
My mother died birthing me—
all her blood
following in my wake.

My skin is my mother's, I'm told.
Flower-fair. Enough fair that Father
scorned all my suitors.
Framed by hair plaited and coiled,
my wan face stares back at me
from the mirror. Too pale.
What's this pure refuses *any* proposal,
white returning every bit of light
back to its source.

Not once did I disobey,
always folding my ivory napkin
beside my plate before leaving
Father's table. Excused, of course.
Each night that table teetered
with pies and savories.
Squatting in its pool of pink,
a half-eaten venison haunch
gleamed with cracked salt.

After I'd been put under
that spell of sleep,
and briar-coils swallowed this house,
it seems a stranger
appeared from the forest to have
his way with me.
He disappeared again, poof,
swallowed back
into bramble-shadow.

Then comes the part of my story
predictable as that metallic taste
venison leaves on my tongue.
Born in a gush
of salty water and blood,
my baby is Father's shame—
her fine skin enough
darker than mine
he'll never see his own face
mirrored in hers. One sharp look,
and he turns away. Never mind.
I love her beyond telling.
My wild woodland bloom.
Sweet fatherless girl.

ALCHEMY

The god's sperm shone
with gold. Nine months later, the birth of twins—
those glories we call a sun and moon,
placed above, to keep the dark away.

Another shower of gold, and a hero was born—
sidereal jewel who strides the night
in northern skies.

Gold into babies.
Those babies into heavenly bodies.
Imagine that.

The poor alchemists. What could they do?
All they ever wanted, really,
was to be female. To have wombs.
So they started with gold. They had to start
with *something.*

I am the consolation begun
before dust, before even the black
drift of seed. An ease
reaching down with white roots.
My embrace surrounds
the blinded stone, every
fat-meated corm.
Far, yes, under the ground,
my swollen nodes
grip clay and shifted silt.

Stories predict red,
silk crinkles fine enough
to be made and erased
by a smile. So be it.
I *do* bloom, and leave
a temple-pod crowned
by a circle of high, shaded
windows. Look into them,
Look out. Beneath lies
a belly swollen with seed
fine as dust—endless
bewitchment, the mending
husk of sleep.

THE MOON RECOUNTS THE BIRTH OF THE SUN

The first twin out of the womb,
I rose, chilled and pale,
busy making my peace with the air—
until I saw my mother still labored.
A huge knot lurched in that belly
I'd so recently left,
shoving first against her ribs,
then toward the knees she clutched.
I watched my brother lunge inside her,
amazed there'd ever been room for me.

For days she strained with that pain,
crying for me to help her,
but what could I do? No way
to wrench my brother from her womb,
nothing to do but stay by her side
until she could wedge
her back and drawn-up knees
between two tree trunks
to push him out.

From the first moment he was, of course,
gorgeous—golden, pink,
glowing with the pulse of heat.
The women gathered to *oooh* and *ahhh*.
Twins—how lovely, they said,
looking from him to me,
careful to skirt the problem of such
unequal light and size.

True. I would become my father's
darling girl, showered with stars,
set by his own hand to plump and dwindle,
to reign in the night sky.
Even so, I have good reason
for being withdrawn.

How can others blame me if I'm chaste?
What do they know about someone
still wrapped in the silver caul
of her mother's pain—my only light gathered,
yes, from another's dazzling face?

DEATH MASK

In this mask of paper-thin gold,
your eyes finally close,
their lids, both upper and lower,
equal in swollen size.

Agamemnon, Son of Atreus,
now that you've offered as sacrifice
your blood's own blood
and sent it streaming across a sea,
now that your Love has emptied
the blood of your own heart
into a rose-scented bath,
each of your eyes
is a golden vulva. The right
belongs to your wife,
hers the passageway of your progeny
into this world. The left to your daughter,
her unbroken sex
the price you paid to ease
passage of a thousand keels.

Your goldsmith has fashioned a likeness
so true we see what would haunt your eyes
if ever your eyes could see again.
Only what's dearest, only gold
can be beaten this thin.

THE MOTHER WHO BECAME A TREE

I'm not silent when my children cry.
I speak what words I can

while they watch
golden hairs appear
between their thin legs,
while they learn the swelling
sleep cannot erase.

They sit in my shade and cry out,
thinking I've left them
here alone
in silence, inside
their tyrannous bodies.

DANAE RECALLS HER UNDOING

I saw a shower of gold.
At the edge of my eye's reach,
a brief glimmer slanted downward,

drifting toward me. Standing inside
the garden wall this morning,
I startled to see

a golden dust
coming from an inky bumblebee
thrumming low and slow

through a streak of early light.
Gold came gliding from its thighs
to catch and glint *on me*—

so heavy was that bee with pollen
it carried, so swollen with lusty
work of the sun.

for Roberto Calasso

A god taught the sun its habits,
how to disappear and reappear,
taught it how to cast the dark
shadow-twin that follows us
wherever we walk.

Skimming a hand along
late winter's stubbled plain,
a goddess left a palm print
of flowers uneven and wild.
Mourning her daughter's absence,
she swept the stain of color
to stubble again.

Inside a fearful girl's body,
a god kindled life,
loosed his gleaming demigods
to live among
us plodders and plotters,
the merely human.

No wonder we search
and wonder, dying to know,
peering at crowds
and into mirrors,
hungry to find in our likeness
a light-bathed face.

The gods once touched the earth,
it's plain. How else

to explain our yearning?
This mortal craving
to glimpse in ourselves
half heaven, half not.

VII

Telltale

ANDRÉ BRETON SHARES HIS MUSE

whose hair is a highway, darkway,
alleyway leading me home.
Whose thoughts are mine and never

my own, another bonfire
gone loose in my brain.
Whose waist matters most to nip

and tuck, bottleneck of desire—
her waist the very wastrel
of daylong dedication.

The ankles of his Muse
are circled with silver egrets, her shoulders
slump to touch stars—

she whose wrist flaunts
a pulse of narcissus, whose fingertips
bloom a camellia's lament.

Her mouth makes a footprint, a tulip,
a swan, whatever makes ready
to speak. Her teeth leave a woodcutter's

rat-a-tat-tat on morning's skin,
her tongue a smear of smoke and varnish,
garland and hallowed reed, she

whose eyelashes mime a thistleburr,
its shadow and salt. Whose eyebrows count
the numbers refusing equation.

INTEGUMENT

Bed of longing, fire alarm
rung from the past,
vowels held in a swing
of dipthong, ambassador
to all foreign tongues.
Its own flask
of murky perfume.

The body's only child,
skin holds itself in a moist,
easy sleep. Not a color, no,
but a shawl of all hues
worn when no other
garment will do.
Pump so deep
as to be past priming.
Friction's light-filled leap.

CALENDARS

In the year of lament, each daybreak
grows into a butterfly,
that thaumaturge moving
from color toward dusk and ash.
Each night of this year
fashions a creature that once
crawled, then paused to wrap itself
in the silk of sleep.

In the year of the basket, all roots
drink the rain a leafy canopy sheds,
so twigs can grow long enough
to be cut and plaited.
Though severed from their source,
nodes still sprout, forcing foliage
to spurt through nozzles of green.
The year's growth ring
croons to the others inside
a weaver's braid.

In the year of the vessel, every anchor
glances toward the bottom.
Stars drag themselves across—rim to rim—
that clockwork of the brimming-bowl sky.
A horizon fills itself eye-high with distance.
Deepened, the pines
grow dense with yearly resin.
Snow agrees to shoulder more and more
of its kind. What's meant to hold
does what it can.

HIS TRANSLATOR SPEAKS TO PESSOA

for Greg Simon

Your steamer trunk is poem-heavy.
Hoard of voices. Jewels drinking from the current
surging unseen.

North of African beaches, south of the Stony Isle
lies your twice-lighted home. From its trees,
green shines.

Your abundance builds a plaza from pleasure,
a headdress of mountains. I transcribe your words
wreathing my head.

In multiples, beauty. Within abundance, the sun
of suns. Wed now, you and I forge
a yellow-dark heart.

BLUE BEE, YOUR ANCIENT CULT CONVENING

You're a hymn whose own wings
do the work of singing—work so rapid
it blurs. Your barb embeds
the world's turgid flesh.

Coming from such a tongue,
the wax of your daily housekeeping
burns with a heady flame.
You are the taper
each indigo altar seeks.

Queen of a depthless hue,
you assemble a hallowed,
shiver-sound—
steady whine of sighs.

Gathering that starry powder
stolen from lazuli, you mark
each devotee's forehead with two,
three vertical streaks,
smears of wide-flung air.

Fever eddies your worshippers.
Your dust clings to their hemlines and cuffs.
They walk with skin brushing against
the stain of visible sky.

REM

The sleep of a breeze telltales
a way toward disaster.

Skin's sleep sounds an alarm
blood-deep, flung into tingling.

Trees dozing in wind
force themselves to dream
that dreamscape
without a place to topple.

Thunder asleep is the roll
of hilly horizon, tumbling along.

The deep sleep of a swan
floats a wish out beyond drowning.

whose light is a sun and a darkness
    blaze-bright, oiled shadow
    the iridescence that floats
    each surface
whose appetite is meat-ready, whose hunger
    grinds to a halt, everything stalled
    in the face of such craving
whose dreams are each an orange
    pulled loose from its skin, unwound
    from the lazy-Susan of doubt
whose malice is magnet to drift and chaff,
    malignant cross-hatches
    blotting me out
whose slippage is slack, lackadaisical
    doozie, the smallest sweetheart chute
    letting me out
whose lexicon skews sideways
    across the page margin to margin—
    the white of margin, the black of ink—
    my magpie dishing it out.

THREE WORDS RECOLLECT
THEIR EARLIER SELVES

Window confesses to once being
the *wind's eye* and sighs a bit,
giving off the hard glint
of remembering such loss.

Admitting to being more than just
part of an eye, *pupil* owns up
to its kinship with learning.
Come from the tiny image
others could see reflected
on its dark surface,
it's also a little one
the right size for school—
a perfect way to name
the place for *seeing*.

Meadow divulges the recipe
for its ancestral brew, mead.
Take stream water begun as rain
feeding wild-eyed flowers.
Add the sweetness those blooms
gave up to bees. Cover
and set aside. For the fizz
of transformation, allow
ample time.

High in legend's sky,
a sun-dragon lolls the clouds—
breathing out the curlicued flame
kindled in its belly. Changing the color
of its skin each minute, the sea of fable
holds water-bound beasts
too far from shore to be seen—
huge salt-worms that surface for air,
roiling, blowing a little foam.

Here and now, an orange-bellied plane
drones through the sky. Amphibious airplane.
This creature masters three of the elements
so well it can wear the color of a fourth
as its skin. To land, the plane takes its pick,
lake or shore, avoiding any live flame
that might ignite the fuel cradled
deep in its steel gut.

Landing on pond-skin
in wetlands nearby, a dragonfly
masters the art of multiple sight,
its faceted eyes broken into a thousand
shining drops. Once a nymph,
it breathed water. In air, its wings
sing a continuo of blur. It eats
tiny creatures in mid flight,
delicate whines caught above earth.
Each second of sunlight its thorax
flashes a glimpse of ocean.
Blue-green fire.

RECLUSE

Lean-to after lean-to he'd built
having given him
blank space to write on,
the old bachelor used every
raw fir board
for a page.

White chalk   yellow chalk
Palmer Method
cursive—
each year another
hammer and nails add-on,
another of his longhand hosannas
at Easter.

Green lumber
and all those resurrections he lauded
have long ago gone.

Nothing to do
now that he's dead
but tear it
all down.

Let the moon   sun   moon—
those telltale scripts—
spill his story,
come spilling in.

Someone must eat from the bowl
filled with death.
Only a man, they say, is fit
to dip from it the spoonfuls of pale pudding.
Only a *he* will do
to empty its sweetness dollop by dollop
so neighbors are finally free
to murmur *Sorry for your troubles*,
to find their wraps buried on the unfamiliar bed
and slip away. A man's job.
Or so they say.

All the world knows who made
what's in that bowl. A woman heats measured milk
over blue flame, drifting sugar
and tapioca grains into that scalding froth.
She lifts some to her tongue to test
for sweetness, stirs until the translucent bubbles
look like the work of a tireless
queen bee. Pouring the finished mass
into a crockery bowl, she carries its weight
out to cool in the pantry. She knows
soon enough there'll be the mother and aunts crying—
those poor dear souls—
handkerchiefs knotted like damp dross
at their eyes. Then will come
the real work of day-to-day grieving.
A woman's job.
Now in her mouth the faint
aftertaste, in her breath
a ghost of vanilla and cream.

FROM THE FIRE BUILT
AT THE HOUSE'S HEARTH

A house doesn't finish being a house
at its roof. It won't end there, can't stop
rising, reaching up to make one more
prayer from the chimney and its pot—
a clay spire aspiring to sky.

That chimney sends smoke and soot
upward, away into wind.
Above the hearth, a throat opens
to guide sister to faraway sister,
sparks toward the waiting stars.

WHILE A CONEFLOWER'S
ORANGE FLORETS SHARPEN THE AIR

Honeybee, half
alive on the flower's spiky dome,
your upper body and head
cluttered with pale, wax-like clumps, you raise
one leg, barely moving.
Wings not.

Bee whose hind legs wear
not a bit of pollen's thick cake,
slow, now you nose
into a floret. Elderbee, encumbered
with the hoary remains
weighing on you.

The blur of your wings—that persistent
high-strung hum—is now
only a sunken dream.
The sky thickens its gray matte.
Rain, on its way. Hard falling.

Still, you forage—exuding
the glue of decay, making yourself a magnet
for scurf. You have brushed
too closely and long
against this world's resiny bloom—
your face already a ghost.
Hive-haunted.

TO THE RIVER LIVING A FEW STREETS AWAY

You're my neighborhood's ocean,
here in your thin, meandering guise.
After you've been mist and cloud
and inland-drubbing rain,
you're this bridge-arced ocean,
this self of yourself
a bird can cross in a few breaths.
You're a sweet sea
feeding trees that darken
your banks with shade.

With this less-salty you,
the moon has no particular pull.
All she can do is merely
paint your skin at night
with her changeling face.
Downhill only, you're here
for a sweet interlude
of one-way sleep, a route back
to awake as your huger self.

IN BEAUTY'S EYE, WHICH IS
THE EYE OF THIS WORLD

To sever a flower from the sun-checkered garden,
to bring its suddenly dying star
close to my gaze,
merely hastens beauty's eye
toward me. Holding its round mirror,
its burst of fleeting light
up to my face, I see myself
widen with acceptance—
me, a pupil to its teaching, reflected
on its own pupil.

I become the sun's
watchful silence, its breakaway, strewn body,
the half-lives of light
descended as dapple through leaves.

AS IF EACH BREATH WERE THE LAST

Each exhalation
is a small seed of sky let go,
headed up—each outbound breath
less rich in what my blood
gleans from air, more laden with what
my lungs release.

That sky-seed I exhale
is made by what I need and take
without greed or thought—
a seed the shape
of what I have, of what
I *have* to give away.

WHEN SPIRIT TRANSFORMS THE BODY

With turquoise arms
I'd gain limbs
veined in a color *other* than blue.

With opal soles
I could wander along
shuffling iridescence.

Topaz could be my eyes,
lapis their lashes,
even butterflies would note
if such eyes stayed
open or shut.

And my mouth—
never mind your mouth
I tell myself
mind what it speaks—
my words could be agates
rolled by ocean salt
mirror-smooth.

VIII

A Darkly Lit Blood

FOR THE SILENCE AMONG AND AROUND WORDS

A cavity-nester, the flicker emerges—
claws tucked, tail trailing—
through the hole only a feather's width larger
than its wing-snugged breast.
A pocket gopher exits through
the body-wide tunnel it dug into dirt.
Water—filling all it can—enters
through the hollow made
by a rock's quarrel with itself.

There, in every tree's trunk, each hillock,
each stone. In every mote, tittle, and dot.
In all who grow wings, in the more who don't.
In toothless ones, in those whose teeth
curve and yellow. In the piece of bread
one bite less than whole, the used ticket
crumpled, torn and tossed aside.
Inside brain cells sputtering whimsy.
There in bodied and bodiless waters.
In all singers, in songs written and not,
lies that emptiness, the hallowed space where
spirit comes in, spirit goes out.

A FLOOR PLAN

One room in your house
is the sky. Not the attic—no,
not such a huddled, slope-ceiling place.
True, you look up, you think of *ascent*
when someone says the air's blue name.
But who ever heard of stooping
to walk in a sky?

Think of your home's largest,
open space. Begin at your feet.
Rising from a floor,
the sky expands to become
intaken breath—air
filled with enough stars to feed
your darkly lit blood.

The glass of sleep beside your bed,
now emptied. What was full
when you lay down to darkness
isn't anymore. Drank it, yes,
you're certain you did,
but hardly *how*. A lip's print
scallops the rim. A last dreg
rings the bottom—yeasty
trace of dream.

What will it do in the daytime,
during your absence,
this glass that held
your night? Nothing
save fill again.

INSIGHT

Risen from a dark
lying beneath
water's deep weight,

grown from a mire
rich with what
fell to the bottom,

fed by what gets
left to sink
far out of sight,

a lotus bud
sunders the pond's skin
to blaze open—

small sun
breaking through
skies of rain.

FONT

Your most ancient kin
were born from the flux
of frenzied suns. You come
from the family *Sky,*
your line of descent
plain in whatever you write
by hand. A telltale cursive.

With the eddied script
that galaxies scrawl
across the night,
you make your mark—
your signature
a dark river of stars.

CODA

The dying tree's branches
are either bare or barely
knobbed with stunted leaves—
except for all the branch-tips
where a last spurt of fresh growth
moves, in a breeze.

On each limb's end, a green
butterfly dries its wings.
Going nowhere. Crazy to fly.

BEDSIDE READING

The too-soon hour
you emptied by waking

fills with the book you earlier
set aside to fall asleep.

What harm in a few more pages
read long before dawn?

On this lamplight lake, held
in the boat of another's making,

you float—lifted, rocked, stolen away.
Buoyed along in a writer's craft.

HOW TO VANISH INTO TODAY'S SKY

Lift into late winter's cold,
the furnace-stung room
left behind you. Send the self
you're ready to expose
up and into that buildup of chill.

Leave, below, the little warmth
sun has pressed into wan grass
and crumbled pavement.
Rise into the blue
that's only blue when it's far.
Be the far—yourself a waywardness
finding its way.

The sky now around you
is your oldest love,
that air you ease in and out
of your body. This is the love
making itself lighter and larger
as you move upward,
requiring from you as you go
deeper and deeper breath.

HERE TO WAIT OUT THE DARK

Surprised by the cold
when last evening's clouded sky
went quickly clear in summer dusk,
you knots of ink and yellow stripes
were caught fast in open blooms,
held overnight in powdery palms.

Little stars come earthly close,
now morning's here. Time to warm you
out of a flower's pollen.
Three, four, five
in a blossom, motionless,
your wings and barbs crimped by dew,
who better than *you* to tell
a story of light slipping over dawn's lip
into the basin of day?

You stir, uncurl, to become
the sun's furious buzzing—
fever flown up, into this world.

IMPRINT

Each day you leave—
wherever you've stepped—
shapes strung along the ground.
Right, left, right, your footprints
are the quick kisses feet steal, a trace
of where your body's been
and been weighty enough to make
an impression— your journey's
own configuration.

Go where you need to.
Step with care. From that earth
left behind you as you walk,
your faint trail shines.

WHY THE ASTILBE'S COLOR FADES

Once a *look-no-farther-than-me* cerise
just one shade this side
of respectable,
its plume of tiny florets
has leached to pale rose mist.

Bees, the bees, all these varied drinkers
come to the party of its blooming.
After sipping a little blush, a bit
of its vegetable blood,
they fly away to feed
the heart of their own making.

INTERCHANGEABLE

Its wing-scales a fabric
soft as lunar dust,
a moth takes direction from only
the moon. With the deep belief
science calls *instinct,* it trusts
in navigation via moonlight,
finding its way by using
what's borrowed from another source.

Your porch light offers
a source of boundless confusion.
Reached it, the moth believes,
then flies past, circles back,
bumps against the hard, slick,
unpredictably warm skin
of this down-to-earth moon.
Past and back, again and again.
Endlessly, until the light
is switched off—by you
or the sun. Either will do.

Position the page
so a small dot of light falls
on the exact space
where your pen now writes.
A wafer of sun travels down
through leaf-breaks in the arbor,
ready to spotlight
lines and loops of ink.

This shining disc becomes
your own moon, sending
what it borrows up to your eyes.
Each word on the page
rises through that light.

TO THE MILKY WAY

Below your swirling gleam,
our city of bridges straddles
a river begun in Cascade snow,
ended in Pacific sea.
Visiting the Willamette at night—
its current only blocks from my house—
I see our neighborhoods giving off
their bottled fire, releasing
mountains of light up, toward you,
enough to keep most of your star-stream
from our eyes.
               Look down,
Celestial River of Unfamiliar Suns.
Find me where I've come to stand
on a bridge's arc, gazing downward
at an earth-river's homeward flow.
Be kind.   Let a few drops of your milk
shine back at me from water's darkened skin.

Owning nothing,
I rent everything
from the world,

whatever I want
costing exactly
what I have.

No calculations,
no ink, red or black.
Never a wait for change.

IX

The Furrier's Next of Kin

Rocks big as the circle of my arms
fringed our backyard flowerbed—
their surface a terrain of tiny pockets.

Just old enough to fill a watering can
by myself, I pointed its spout
and poured into each willing basin.

Dotted with lakes, a stony wilderness
then bordered our Johnny-jump-ups,
our sun-white Shasta daisies.

I stayed close. I waited.
Animals smaller than imagining
came to the edges and drank.

SHOWROOM

At the Five & Dime, stacked tablets
framed the same Indian's face
on every cover—their fifty sheets
the pulpy beige of skins, underside
of the animal pelts piled high, across town,
in my grandpa Archie's fur shop.
Blue lines ruled the tablet pages, ready
to channel what I would write.

Veins had once lined those bodies—
feeding their eyes, claws, their sharp,
hard snouts. Some women wore a string
of whole pelts fastened jaw to tail,
as if minks or kolinskies
had bitten each other to death circling
their shoulders. The square-shouldered chief
sported a bonnet of long feathers.
Finely curved, starkly white,
they carried puffs of down near their base.
Each time I opened the tablet to write,
I turned his face over and under.

Running fingers over the soft fur,
a woman tried on a whole-pelt stole
in Archie's showroom. A glass eye
stared from each dry socket.
From the tablet-chief's brow
plumes rose and spread out
in a giant fan. Tail feathers.
He had shot—with arrows
launched from his bow—bald eagles,
wrenching prizes from their downed bodies,

each quill-tip oozing
a drop of blood. I'd never seen
a live eagle, its yellow eyes.

The customer eyed herself
in the tall, three-way mirror while Archie
watched her. Both looked pleased.
The woman had a feral gleam
to fling around the padded shoulders
of her new fall suit. Beige worsted.
She wrote Archie a check, spilling
her name onto that thin bottom line.
I began to see. Blue lines would carry
my blood too, from page to page.

WHAT THE SHAMAN KNEW,
WHAT MY GRANDFATHER THE FURRIER
WOULDN'T HAVE KNOWN TO DO
WITH THE WHOLE OTTERSKIN
USED AS A MEDICINE BAG:

To bead the underside of its tail—
that long V from anus to final tip—
with eagle shapes. To cover its paws,
their crescents of claw, with beaded flaps.

Just inside the otter's wizened mouth,
to affix tufts of red floss
so they burst from its muzzle.
No one would dare claim
because a trapper delivered the pelt
drawn and scraped,
there'd been no blood.

Faced with that emptiness
any furrier would fill with glass eyes—
an amber centered by pools of darkness—
my grandfather could never have known
to stay his hand as the shaman did, to leave
the sockets raw. Entirely blind.

A boy brings snapshots to show me—
not a bad boy, mind you. There, he points,
it's him hunkered behind his first bobcat,
his fingers lifting its head by tufted ears
so the camera can get a good shot.
And here he is with a brace of mallards,
his hand circling their necks, their bodies
hanging like two soft sacks.

A nice enough boy, really, here he is
standing in front of his square of house, grinning.
In front of him, seven Canada geese lie
breast down, arranged in a V
on the pale thatch of November lawn—
wings pried open into motionless flight,
each neck straightened. Their bills all point
in this direction, toward some spot
on the two-dimensional landscape
dead ahead, just out of sight.

A RECIPE FOR ABSTENTION

I dream of wolf meat sizzling
in a cast iron pan.
Pin-prick of greased heat
tattooing my hands.
I know this smell. No one need say aloud
vanishing or *struck bargain*
for me to understand.

Feral-full, my lungs
sear and smart—even though
a long-handled fork and its sharp tines
give distance between
me and what I turn in the pan.

A closed mouth seals the wound
of all I've ever blurted.
My lips press hunger's honed edge
back into my gut.

MECHANISTICS

Near the place we sleep,
a creature blinks away the darkness,
calling to us in thin cries
when our version of daybreak
arrives. We invite one—
miniature, exotic—to live
under our skin, high on our chest,
implore it to make our heart
speak an even, predictable beat,
ask another to press its ear against our ribs,
listening for what pulses within.

One whose body we've entered
courses street to street, city to city,
that whine of its touch on pavement
our prayer, high and sustained.
We command them: teach us
to fly, hover, to swim for miles
without a drop of water
cooling our skin. Subdue for us
the wild and furred, those blood-filled,
ancient kind. Be our answer
to what we believe we need,
be what we design.

Watching a child at play—
one absorbed to the point of worship
by such a creature clad in bright enamel,
such a one made simple, made small—
we can sense what children surely know.
Here is something to take apart,
to reassemble with logic's steady whir.

Machines are those animals
we create, then can ruin, the ones
we need not slow our pace to grieve.

Lady Day's voice thrums from inside.
Honey-slow dusk moves onto the porch
where a woman's come to sit, watching
a neighbor's Herefords in the stubble field
a few feet away. Their fleshy noses
pushed through the wire fence,
they can't get enough of the quack grass
growing rank and sharp on her side,
can't get enough of watching her
lift a glass to her mouth and set it down.
They bunch, stare, shoulder in, their perfectly
solid bodies bending the fence until

she thinks she could reach out
and touch them if she tried. *No use, none.*
Tonight she'll stand at the stove,
her husband leaning into her back,
pressing her against the edge, his hands
under her blouse, on her breasts,
his voice against her hair—in play,
in love, in praise of the meat
she spoons onto a thick, white plate.

TRANSACTION

The butcher's knife was sharp.
It severed a chunk from its source
so cleanly it seemed nothing
was taken or left.
His saw whined so evenly
circles of bone
looked healed, whole—
each cut of meat blooming as if
sprung from only itself.

He weighed our choice,
then laid it on a sheet of paper,
flawless, where into his flourish
of creases and folds
it disappeared.
Cool to the touch,
what we carried away
might have been *anything*.
White, sealed—as if we could
keep this bargain yet leave
not a smudge of blood,
no trace of our hands.

CONVERSION

When religion was based on meat,
we worshipped on the run.
Our purpose an arrow,
we pursued—
hot on the trail
of anything warm.

A simple hit or miss,
no mystery in that.
But something went wrong.
Halfway to paradise,
our palate broke down.

Tired of gristle
stuck between our teeth,
we set our mouths
on food of a thornier kind—
bare-of-bone staples.
A nip of bread, sip of wine.

PAWNEE STAR-CHART

A forest-heart beating in darkness,
an antlered head bedded, asleep.
Sifting down through tree tops,
through understory,
gleam from a night sky
dapples its rump, speckles its withers.
As these bits of light move
in patterns on its bristled skin,

a way emerges for mapping the sky.

In white cross-marks, constellations
will some day be painted
on its stretched and softened hide.
A deer passes through this one world
only to enter it again.
Stars find a way to shine
once more—a sky's light
borne twice on an animal's back.

Not even noon and my feet are thick
with dust and heat. I stand
at the pedestal sink, placing first one foot
and then another
into the faucet's stream,
balancing like a shorebird—
one leg planted square to the floor,
the other crooked, knee to my chest.

An egret far from home,
I'm pale, almost white in this land
of olive bodies sun-browned
darker, deep. Heat riddles my skin
with discontent. It won't relent.
Bells from the Church of Metamorphosis
tell their story of ten, eleven,
highest noon. Height of sun.
The day's light stands straight up,
it floods straight down.

Land of heat, say the bells,
realm of swollen sun. No room
for a moon to hang its smudge of light
in daytime sky. No place for a pale
moon-bird to hide.

DIRECTION

for Sara Halprin

Only her loved ones
are sure we've found our way—
the way to get lost being so easy
that a van led our chain of cars
uphill to this grave marker
covered with green cloth glaring
against November's still-fresh grass.

Gathered into a wavery circle
around the concealed stone,
we stand on sloping lawn so steep
we each dig one heel in
to keep from toppling.
The Rabbi plays his guitar, he sings,
those knowing Hebrew follow along,
the rest of us give it a try.

Below us the hill levels out
to a brief meadow before finishing
its fall to the river. Emerged
from firs on the edge, a deer finds her way
across the clearing—
dark shine of her eyes lifted,
ears swung out and up to our song.

The uphill half of us sees her, the others
ease around when we point.
They look and sigh.

Now the Rabbi lifts
the green grave-cloth. Flat granite gleams
with the name we expect. *Sara*
We aren't lost, after all.
He offers a bowl
filled with polished black stones.

Atop Sara's marker
each of us places a drop of that night
found in a doe's eye.

TO MERELY LOOK, TO PASS ON BY

Antayla, Turkey

A white rabbit and her kits—
the miniatures drawn from herself
and some long-gone buck—
sit on a high table so small, the powder of their fur
sifts over its varnished edges.
This bait, this lure waits
on the promenade that traces a horseshoe
of Mediterranean coastline.

Once I've let myself touch,
the man standing beside the rabbits will want
my lira. A million or two
for the fortune on a small strip of paper—
told, of course, in the Turkish
I don't understand—
he'll press into my palm.

My hand is drawn.
The hand of each nearby child
draws out of a parent's nest-hand
toward this white bliss
soft as newborn sleep.

As I walk by, my breath
releases its slow sigh. Praise for long ears
lined with blush.
For the deep world flushed
pink with blood.

My bones will grow hollow, slight.
I'll become so light sun will flow
right through me, my skin a thin-spun
window, transparent husk.

Liver, kidneys, double bulb of lungs,
intestine's meander, all will be gone.
My entire trunk will empty then be filled
with the face of my animal-soul,
its silky cheek fur, glinted whiskers,
huge eyes and snout.

Nothing left of the earthbound middle-me
but a gut heat, not a thing but—
midway in the animal brow—
my heart beating.

AND WHERE DOES IT COME FROM, THIS ANIMAL-SOUL?

From inside the echoing rooms
of my grandfather's fur shop.
Bit by bit. I was young,
the fur was sleek, soft. I didn't know.
Even the stiffest guard hairs gleamed.
My animal-soul pieced itself together each time
I touched a pelt.

My grandfather wet down the skins
and with fine, needle-tipped nails stretched them
on a pine board. Their musk rivered
into my breath. On her black enameled machine,
Nana sewed linings of satin to conceal
each soft-napped underside.

For too long, I didn't realize
what my fingers had gathered into me
mote by mote as I grew. The sorrow, those eyes
caught in blinding light,
a leg only half bitten in half
by a trap's metal jaw.

My animal-soul has countless names.
Blue fox, red fox, silver.
Ermine, beaver, fitch.
I was a child then. *I did know.*
A terrible beauty had found me.
Seal and cony and karakul. My hands
reach for them all.

ACKNOWLEDGEMENTS

With gratitude to the editors of the following publications, in which some of the *Understory* poems appeared or are forthcoming:

The Alembic • *Atlanta Review* • *Bear Deluxe* • *Calapooya Collage* • *Calyx* • *Carolina Quarterly* • *Clackamas Literary Review* • *Clover* • *Fireweed* • *The Florida Review* • *The Grove Review* • *Heliotrope* • *High Desert Journal* • *Hubbub* • *The Inflectionist* • *Manzanita Quarterly* • *The Monarch Review* • *Oregon English Journal* • *Pacific Review* • *Poetry Northwest* • *Portland* • *Portland Review* • *Rhonde Dance* • *Sequoia* • *Spoon River Poetry Review* • *Take-Out* • *Toe Good Poetry* • *Untitled Country* • *VoiceCatcher* • *Weber Studies* • *West Wind Review* • *Windfall*

With gratitude to the editors of the following chapbooks, artist's book, and anthologies in which some of the *Understory* poems appeared or are forthcoming:

The Animal Bride (Trask House Books)

The Art of Angling, Poems about Fishing (Everyman's Library Pocket Poets)

A Blue Grown Deep Enough & Barely a Thread (Paul Merchant)

Dark River of Stars, a collaboration with Barbara Mason and Laurie Weiss (Black Dog Studio)

Fabrication (26 Books)

Honoring Our Rivers 2012 (Willamette Partnership)

Motionless from the Bridge (Bare bone books)

In Our Own Voices (Oregon Writers Colony)

Peace, Peace, to the Far and to the Near (Trinity Episcopal Church)

Shimmer and Drone (Imperfect Press)

These Mountains That Separate Us (Traprock Books)

"Capital" is featured on the Peace Mosaic in Salem, Oregon (artistic director, Lynn Takata).

"Raga" appeared as a broadside from Imperfect Press, designed by Beth C. Ford.

"Danae Recalls Her Undoing" will appear as a limited edition broadside designed and letterpress printed by Carla Girard, Mercuria Press.